P9-CAS-856

The Art of Intermittent Fasting

How to Lose Weight, Shed Fat, and Live a Healthier Life

By Connor Thompson

Table of Contents

© Copyright 2018 by Connor Thompson - All rights reserved.

The following eBook is reproduced below with the goal of providing information that is as accurate and reliable as possible. Purchasing this eBook can be seen as consent to the fact that both the publisher and the author of this book are in no way experts on the topics discussed within and that any recommendations or suggestions that are made herein are for entertainment purposes only. Professionals should be consulted as needed prior to undertaking any of the actions endorsed herein.

This declaration is deemed fair and valid by both the American Bar Association and the Committee of Publishers Association and is legally binding throughout the United States.

Furthermore, the transmission, duplication, or reproduction of any of the following work, including specific information, will be considered an illegal act irrespective of if it is done electronically or in print. This extends to creating a secondary or tertiary copy of the work or a recorded copy and is only allowed with an expressed written consent from the Publisher. All additional rights reserved.

The information in the following pages is broadly considered to be a truthful and accurate account of facts and as such any inattention, use, or misuse of the information in question by the reader will render any resulting actions solely under their purview. There are no scenarios in which the publisher or the original author of this work can be, in any fashion, deemed liable for any hardship or damages that may befall readers after undertaking information described herein.

Additionally, the information in the following pages is intended only for informational purposes and should thus be thought of as universal. As befitting its nature, it is presented without assurance regarding its prolonged validity or interim quality. Trademarks that are mentioned are done without written consent and can in no way be considered an endorsement from the trademark holder.

Introduction

Congratulations and thank you for downloading this eBook.

The following chapters will discuss everything that you need to know to get started with intermittent fasting. This is a great diet plan that focuses more on the time to eat foods as opposed to the actual food you are eating. There are many different options when it comes to using the intermittent fast, so you will be able to make it work for your lifestyle.

This guidebook will provide you with all the information that you need to get started with an intermittent fast. We will look at what this fast is all about, the health benefits that come with it, how to eat on this diet plan, and much more. We will also answer some common questions about fasting so that you are fully prepared to get started.

The intermittent fast is a great option for those who currently have or have had trouble losing weight and who want something that will work well for them. Make sure to check out this guidebook to help you to get started with intermittent fasting today.

There are plenty of books on this subject out on the market, so thanks again for choosing this one. Every effort was made to ensure that it is packed full of useful information, so please enjoy!

Chapter 1: How Our Modern Diet is Failing Us

We all know that we need to eat healthier. We also know that we need to limit how much soda, juice, processed foods, and sugars that we consume. However, even though we know these things, it doesn't mean that it is as easy to follow.

According to a recent food and health survey done by Psychology Today, 52 percent of Americans believe that it is easier for them to figure out their taxes than it is to figure out how to eat healthily. Plenty of people have trouble with the current tax code, which means that even more people are having trouble figuring out how to eat a diet that is good for them.

We live in a country that is fighting a battle with obesity. More than a third of the US population is considered obese, and many are also considered overweight. However, these statistics do not show the complete picture. For example, two out of three adults are considered either overweight or obese, meaning that most people will fall into this category.

Why are these statistics so dismal? There are a lot of factors that contribute to obesity, and one big culprit is the standard American diet. There has been a huge decrease in the quality of our diets as we have gone from a nation that relied on food from local farms to a nation that mass-produces most of our food. In turn, this transition has increased our food consumption because it is so readily available now.

Additionally, many foods that are readily available and easy to make are high in fat, sugars, and calories, all of which contribute to weight gain. From the sugary snacks that we find in the break room to all the fast food chains that are around us, the quality of food and the amount we eat has changed drastically. We could literally eat unhealthy foods non-stop if we wanted to which is why obesity is so prevalent in our culture.

The first thing we should look at is the quantity of food that we are eating. The number of calories that each person needs varies from person to person. Factors include genetics, activity level, overall health, height, age, and gender. However, the benchmark number that is used on food labels is about 2,000 calories each day. This number is already fairly high for those who live a sedentary life, yet it is also possible to eat 2,000 calories (or more) in just one sitting if you go out to eat or order food in.

While eating out quickly pushes us past our calorie limits, it is also possible to eat more even when we eat at home. It is important to learn how to start eating what we need to function rather than eating because something tastes good or because we are bored, tired, or sad.

To calculate the average amount of daily calories that are consumed by Americans, organizations examine the amount of food available per person as indicators for the amount of food that is consumed. In the United States, this ends up being around 3,800 calories each day. Even when you account for the fact that some of this food is wasted or discarded each day, the average American still consumes 2,700 calories each day which is way more than anyone needs, even if they are leading an active lifestyle, which many Americans are not.

It is important to also discuss the quality of the food that most Americans eat. Growing up, most of us learn from our parents and teachers which foods are good and which ones are not. Fruits and vegetables are seen as "good" while sugars and sweets are "bad". Simialrly, the rest of the foods may not have been as good for you, but they were thought to be fine in moderation. Even though we were taught about healthy eating at a young age, in practice, it is much harder to follow this advice.

According to the U.S. Department of Agriculture, the top six sources of calories for most Americans are grain-based desserts, yeast breads, chicken, soda, sports and energy drinks, and alcoholic beverages. Note that fruits and vegetables are not listed. This means that out of this top five list, most of the foods that Americans consume are refined grains and sugars. It is estimated that only eight percent of the average American diet consists of fruits and vegetables.

According to a study done by the United States Department of Agriculture (USDA) in 2010, nuts, meats, and eggs make up 21% of these diets, oils and fats make up 23%, and caloric sweeteners make up 15%. Combined, this means that the foods that are not that good for us makes up a good 61 % of our diets.

The time of day that we eat can matter as well. Most Americans live a busy lifestyle so they do not have the time to sit down and eat well-balanced meals. Instead, they eat on the go, usually at some place that is unhealthy, or they eat at night when their metabolisms are slower. Additionally, many

Americans spend their free time sitting on the couch and eating unhealthy snack foods while watching television. Sometimes, food is so abundant that we eat non-stop.

It is important to learn the necessary steps to limit how much food we are taking in each day. It is tempting to eat foods that are easily available, but if you want to regain your health and stay in good shape, it is important to step away from the typical American diet and choose something that is healthier and better for you.

When you hear the word, "fasting", you might think of people who go for weeks without eating due to religious reasons. You might even think that it is unhealthy or that you won't be able to do it since you love food too much. However, intermittent fasting is different from religious fasting, although they do share some common ideas.

Intermittent fasting is about restricting your caloric intake during certain parts of the day or simply not eating as much on certain days. Your body still gets the nutrients it needs, but you eat fewer calories, therefore making it is easier to lose weight. Some of the different types of intermittent fasting will be discussed later on in the book.

The reason why this diet is successful is that it is effective at reducing the amount of fat that is in your body as well as the number of calories that you are consuming. Since you are reducing the time frame in which you are allowed to eat or are lowering your caloric intake on certain days of the week, it is much easier to lower your overall calorie count.

You can also choose how long you would like to do the intermittent fast. Some people choose to do it for a month or more while others fit it into their lifestyles, sticking with it long term.

Chapter 2: What is Intermittent Fasting

Now that we have taken some time to look at how the American diet is making us unhealthy, let's look a diet that will make it easier to lose weight and become healthier. This chapter will discuss what intermittent fasting is all about so that you can understand how it may work for you.

Intermittent fasting consists of a dieter cycling between periods when people are allowed to eat and periods where they are supposed to fast. This type of diet doesn't necessarily say which foods you can eat, but it does specify when you should eat. Of course, if you want to lose weight or become healthier, it is better to eat foods that are not only good for you, but that are also nutritious.

There are different types of intermittent fasting methods, but all of them split up your day or week into eating periods and fasting periods. What you may be surprised to know is that most of us already fast each day when we are sleeping, and intermittent fasting simply extends the natural fast time. For example, you may decide to skip breakfast and have your first meal at noon and your last meal at 8 pm. This would be considered a form of intermittent fasting.

With this method, you are technically fasting for sixteen hours each day and only eat during an eight-hour period of the day. This form of fasting, also known as the 16/8 method, is one of the popular options when it comes to intermittent fasting.

Despite what you may be thinking right now, intermittent fasting is actually easier than you think.

It doesn't take much planning and countless people who have gone on this diet report that they feel better and have more energy when they are on a fast. In the beginning, you may struggle a bit with hunger, but it won't take long before your body adapts and gets used to it.

The main thing to remember when you are in the fasting period is that you are not allowed to eat. You can, however, still drink beverages to keep you hydrated. Some of the options include tea, coffee, water, and other non-caloric beverages. Some forms of this fast will allow for a bit of food during the fasting periods, but most don't. Additionally, it is usually fine to take supplements while you are on this fast, long as they don't contain calories.

Why Fast?

The next question that you may have is, "Why should I consider fasting in the first place?" For starters, humans have been going through periods of fasting for many years. They sometimes did this out of necessity since they were not able to find any food to eat, but there were also times that fasting was done for religious reasons. Religions such as Buddhism, Christianity, and Islam mandate some form of fasting. Finally, it is natural to fast when you are feeling sick.

Although fasting sometimes has a negative connotation, there is nothing that is unnatural about fasting. In fact, our bodies are well equipped to handle times when we have to go without eating. There are quite a few processes inside of the body that change when we go on a fast which help our bodies to continue functioning during periods of famine.

When we fast, we get a significant reduction in insulin and blood sugar levels, as well as a drastic increase in what is known as the human growth hormone. While this is something that originally occurred when food was scarce, it is now used to help people lose weight. With fasting, burning fat becomes simple, easy, and effective.

Some people decide to go on a fast because it can help their metabolism; this kind of fasting can help improve various health disorders and diseases. There is also some evidence that shows how intermittent fasting can help you to live longer. For example, recent studies have shown that rodents were able to extend their lifespan with intermittent fasting.

Other research shows that fasting can help protect against various diseases such as Alzheimer's, cancer, Type-2 diabetes, and heart disease. There are people who choose to go on an intermittent fast because it's convenient for their lifestyle. Fasting can be a really effective life hack in that the fewer meals you have to make, the simpler your life will become.

Why Does Intermittent Fasting Work?

Intermittent fasting is the practice of scheduling your meals in order for your body to get the most out of them. Rather than cutting your calorie intake in half, depriving yourself of all the foods you enjoy, or diving into a trendy diet fad, intermittent fasting is a simple, logical, and healthful way of eating that promotes fat loss. There are many ways to approach intermittent fasting, but it's simply defined as a specific eating pattern. This method focuses on changing when you eat, rather than what you eat.

When you begin intermittent fasting, you will most likely keep your calorie intake the same, but rather than spreading your meals throughout the day, you will eat bigger meals during a shorter time frame. For example, rather than eating 3 to 4 meals a day, you might eat one large meal at 11 am and another at 6 pm. The idea is that you will eat no meals in between 11 am and 6 pm or between 6 pm and 11 am the next day. This is only one method of intermittent fasting. While others will be detailed in this book in later chapters, you must first understand why this method works.

Intermittent fasting is a method utilized by many bodybuilders, athletes, and fitness gurus to keep their muscle mass high and their body fat percentage low. It is a simple strategy that allows you to eat the foods you enjoy while still promoting fat loss and muscle gain or maintenance. Intermittent fasting can be practiced short term or long term, but the best results come from adopting this method into your everyday lifestyle.

Though the word "fasting" may alarm the average person, intermittent fasting does not equate to starving yourself. To understand the principals behind successful intermittent fasting, we'll first go over the body's two states of digestion: the fed state and the fasting state.

For three to five hours after eating a meal, your body enters what is known as the "fed state." During the fed state, your insulin levels increase to absorb and digest your food. When your insulin levels are high, it is difficult for your body to burn fat. Insulin is a hormone produced by the pancreas to regulate glucose levels in the bloodstream. Though its purpose is to regulate, insulin is technically a storage hormone. So, when insulin levels are high, this means that your body is burning your food for energy rather than stored fat. Therefore, increased insulin levels actually prevent weight loss.

Once the three to five hours are up, your body has finished processing the meal and you enter the post-absorptive state. The post-absorptive state lasts anywhere from 8 to 12 hours, and it is after this time gap that your body enters the fasted state. Since your body has completely processed your food by this point, your insulin levels are low, making your stored fat extremely accessible for burning.

In the fasted state, your body has no food left to utilize for energy, so your body burns stored fat instead. Intermittent fasting allows your body to reach an advanced fat burning state that you would normally reach with the average eating pattern of three meals per day. This factor alone is the reason why many people notice rapid results with intermittent fasting without even making changes to their exercise routines, how much they eat, or what they eat; they are simply changing the timing and pattern of their food intake.

When you begin an intermittent fasting program, it may take some time to get into the swing of things, but don't get discouraged! If you slip up, just get back into your intermittent fasting pattern whenever you can. Most importantly, avoid beating yourself up or feeling guilty as negative self-talk will only prolong you getting back to your pattern. Making a lifestyle change takes a conscious effort and no one expects you to do it perfectly right away. If you are not used to going for long periods without eating, intermittent fasting will take some getting used to. As long as you choose the right method for you, stay focused, and remain positive, you will get the hang of it in no time.

Unlike other diet plans that you may go on, the intermittent fast is one that will work. It uses your body and how it works to its advantage to help you to lose weight. It is easy to get a bit scared when you hear about fasting. You may assume that you need to spend days and weeks without eating (and who really has the willpower to give up their food for that long even when they do want to lose weight?) but naturally, that it will be too hard for you.

Intermittent fasting is a bit different than you may imagine. Not only is it really hard to go on a fast for weeks at a time, but it is also not good for the body, and oftentimes, your body will enter starvation mode if you end up fasting for too long. This is because your body assumes that you are in a time without much food so it will work on saving as many calories as possible, helping you to hold on to the fat and calories for as long as possible. This means that you are not only hungry, but that you are also missing out on losing weight.

You don't have to get too worried about this because you are not going to fast for so long that your body goes into this starvation mode and stops losing weight. Instead, it will make the fast last just long enough that you will be able to speed up the metabolism. That's what makes it effective.

With the intermittent fast, you will find that when you go for a few hours without eating (usually no more than about 24 hours), the body is not going to go right into starvation mode. Rather, it is going to consume the calories that are available. If you ate the right number of calories for the day, your body is going to revert to eating up the stored reserves of fat and use it as fuel. As such, when following an intermittent fasting plan, you are forcing your body to burn more fat without putting in any extra work.

Here are few quick tips for success:

First and foremost, it is important that you not expect to see results from your new lifestyle immediately. Instead, you need to plan on committing to the process for at least 30 days before you can start to accurately judge the results.

Second, it is important to keep in mind that the quality of the food you put into your body still matters as it will only take a few fast food meals to undo all of your hard work.

Finally, for the best results, you will want to incorporate a light exercise routine during your fasting days along with a more traditional routine for your non-fasting days.

Types of Intermittent Fasting

There are a few major types of intermittent fasting that you can choose to work with. These fasts can all be effective, and the one that's right for you will depend on your personal preferences, schedule, and lifestyle. Some of the fasting options that you can go with include:

- The 16/8 method: This one will ask you to fast for 16 hours each day and eat during the other 8 hours. So, you may choose to only eat from 12 pm to 8 pm or from 10 am to 6 pm. You can choose whichever eight-hour window that you like.

- Eat-Stop-Eat: Once or twice each week, you will not eat anything from dinner one day until dinner the next day. This gives you a 24-hour fast while still allowing you to eat on each of the days that you are fasting.

- The 5:2 diet: You will pick out two days of the week to fast. During those two days, you are only allowed to have up to 500-600 calories each day.

Of course, there are variations of the three that are listed above. For example, some people decide to limit their windows even more and only eat for four hours a day and fast for twenty while intermittent fasting. Most people who go on these fasts will choose to go with the 16/8 method because it's the easiest to stick with and will give you some great results in the process.

Intermittent fasting is simple and effective. It helps you limit the calories that you are consuming and burn more fat and calories than you would with a traditional diet.

Chapter 3: How Can I Fast?

One thing that a lot of people like about intermittent fasting is that it provides you with a lot of choices. As mentioned previously, there are a few different ways that you can do an intermittent fast based on your schedule and lifestyle. Some people find that they have a few busy days during the week and so will fast on those days. Others like the idea of limiting their eating window and doing a small fast each day.

The fasting method that you choose is up to you, but they can all effective and will provide you with some of the benefits that you are looking for. Let's look at some of the fasting options that you can choose from so that you can choose the right one for you.

The 16/8 Method

This is one of the most common methods that you can use when intermittent fasting. It requires that you fast for 14 to 16 hours each day and eat during the remainder of the hours. During this eating window, you are still able to fit in two to three meals without a problem. This is more likely to fit into the eating schedule that you are used to while still limiting you so that you do not eat all day long.

This method is easier than you think. It is as easy as not eating any snacks after you are done with dinner and then skipping breakfast, or at least having a late breakfast. So, if you finish your last meal at 8 pm and then do not eat anything until noon the next day, you are already fasting for 16 hours. You just have to be careful about the late-night snacks, but if you eat them, you will simply need to avoid breakfast in the morning.

Some people have issues with this because they feel hungry in the morning and feel they need to eat breakfast. If this is the case, you can simply eat your breakfast a little later in the day. For example, if you choose to eat breakfast at 10 am instead of 8 amand then stop eating by 6 pm, you would still be within the 16-hour window.

If you're a woman, this is the option that you should probably go with as women typically do the best with shorter fasts. In fact, some may even want to consider fasting 14 to 15 hours between meals because this is more effective for them.

During the fast, you are allowed to drink water, tea, coffee, and other beverages that are non-caloric to help reduce the hunger pangs that occur. Additionally, you should try to stick with healthier foods during your eating window. It is not a good idea to eat a lot of unhealthy food during this time. Some people like to go on a low-carb diet when they are on intermittent fast because it helps with hunger and allows for better results.

The 5:2 Diet

Another option that you can go with is the 5:2 diet. This one asks you to eat normally for five days during the week and restrict yourself to no more than 600 calories on the other two days. This is sometimes called "the fast diet" as well.

On these fasting days, it is recommended that women stay around 500 calories and men at 600 calories. For instance, you will eat normally each day of the week, but on Mondays and Thursdays, you will only eat two small meals with a total of 500-600 calories. You can choose any days of the week as your fasting days as long as you don't have them back to back. Pick your two busiest days of the week and make those your fasting days.

There are not many studies out there about the 5:2 diet, but since it is an intermittent fast, it will provide most of the benefits that you are looking for. You will be able to get things done without having to worry about making meals the whole day.

Eat-Stop-Eat Diet

The Eat-Stop-Eat diet requires that you refrain from eating for 24 hours once or twice a week. This method was first popularized by Brad Pilon and has been a popular way to do the intermittent fast for some time. It's possible to follow this fast while still having one meal a day. Most people will have supper one day and then not eat anything until supper the next day. This method allows you to never go an entire day without eating while still falling in the 24-hour abstinence period.

You can change this however you like. For example, if it is easier for you to go from breakfast to breakfast or lunch to lunch, then you can choose one of these options. During your fast, you are allowed to have coffee, water, and other non-caloric beverages to keep yourself hydrated, but you're not allowed to have any food.

Remember that you are only fasting for one or two days a week. So, when it's time to eat normally, you will need to eat the same amount of food that you would have if you were not on a fast. This will help you to lose weight without harming your body.

The biggest issue with going on this kind of intermittent fast is that fasting for 24 hours is hard for most people. However, you can ease into it. You may find that starting with a shorter fast, such as the 16-hour fast, can provide some good results. Then, you can start fasting for longer periods of time. Going an entire day without eating can be tough, so most people choose to go with one of the other fasting options to see the same results.

Alternate Day Fasting

With this option, you will go on a fast every other day. There are a few options that you can go with, and it will depend on what works for your needs. Some of these fasts will allow you to have about 500 calories on your fasting days. You will find that many studies concerning intermittent fasting used some version of the alternate day fast to help determine all the health benefits.

Fasting every other day can be difficult for most people and is something that you will probably need to build up to. You will likely feel really hungry several times a week on this fasting plan, and it is hard to stick with long-term.

Warrior Diet

This is another popular option that you can choose when it comes to intermittent fasting and involves eating small amounts of raw fruits and vegetables during the day followed by a large meal at night. This diet requires you to fast all day, eating just enough to keep you satisfied, and then feasting at night within a four-hour eating window.

The warrior diet was one of the first "official" diets to incorporate some form of intermittent fasting. The warrior diet also includes food choices that mimic the Paleo diet. You will not only fast for most of the day and feast at night, but you will eat a diet that is full of unprocessed foods that resemble what you can find out in nature.

Spontaneous Meal Skipping

You can try this if you want to prepare your body for intermittent fasting or if you don't want to spend much time worrying about when you can eat. With this fast, you do not need to worry about following one of the more structured intermittent fasting plans as you will just skip some meals from time to time. You can do this when you are not hungry or when you are just too busy to have a meal.

It is a myth that you have to eat something every few hours to avoid starvation as the body is well adapted to go for long periods of time without eating. Missing out on a few meals, especially if you are not hungry or too busy, is not harmful to your body.

Any time that you end up skipping a meal or two, you are technically fasting. If you are too busy to grab breakfast on the way out the door, just make sure that you eat a healthy lunch and dinner. If you are out running errands and you are not able to find someplace to eat, then it is fine to miss out on a meal. This practice will not cause you any harm and can actually help you save time.

You probably won't see as good of results compared to some of the other options, but it is better than nothing and is a lot easier to work with. To try it out, skip a meal or two during the week or miss some meals when it works best for you.

As you can see, there are several different options that you can work with when you are ready to go on an intermittent fast. Some of these will be easier than others, and some may fit your schedule better. You will need to choose which fast is easiest for you to work within your daily life.

Chapter 4: Why Should I Try Intermittent Fasting?

There are many different diet plans that you can choose from. Some help you limit your carb intake and focus on the good fats and proteins and others will limit your fat intake while focusing on good and healthy carbs.

With all of the choices on the market, and with at least a few of them being legitimate options for losing weight, you may be curious as to why you should go with intermittent fasting. This chapter will take a look at the various benefits of intermittent fasting and how it will make a difference in your health.

Changes the Function of Hormones, Genes, and Cells

When you do not eat for some time, several things happen to your body. For example, your body will start initiating processes for cell repair and change some of your hormone levels, which makes stored body fat easier to access. Other changes that can happen in the body include:

- Insulin levels: Your insulin levels will drop quite a bit, which will make it easier for the body to burn fat
- Human growth hormone: The blood levels of the growth hormone can greatly increase and higher levels of this hormone can help build muscle and burn fat
- Cellular repair: The body will start important cellular repair processes such as removing all the waste from cells
- Gene expression: Some beneficial changes occur in several genes that will help you to live longer and protect against disease

Lose Weight and Body Fat

Many people go on an intermittent fast to lose weight. In most cases, intermittent fasting will naturally help you to eat fewer meals. Ultimately, you will end up taking in fewer calories, which will lead to weight loss.

Additionally, fasting enhances the hormone function to facilitate weight loss. Higher growth hormone levels and lower insulin help your body to break down fat and use it for energy. This is why short-term fasting can increase your metabolism by at least three percent.

On one side, it boosts your metabolic rate so that you burn more calories while also reducing how much you eat. According to a 2014 review of scientific research on intermittent fasting, people were able to lose up to eight percent of their body weight in less than 24 weeks.

Helps with Diabetes

Type-2 diabetes is a disease that has become widespread in recent decades. Anything that reduces your insulin resistance should help lower your blood sugar levels and protect you against type 2 diabetes. Some studies show how intermittent fasting can benefit people via insulin resistance and can help lead to a dramatic reduction in blood sugar levels.

In several studies on intermittent fasting, blood sugar was reduced by three to six percent, while insulin was reduced by twenty to thirty-one percent. One study on diabetic rats also showed that intermittent fasting was able to protect the rat against kidney damage, a common complication with more serious forms of diabetes. This shows that intermittent fasting may be a good option for anyone with a higher risk of developing type 2 diabetes.

There are, however, some differences between the sexes. There is one study that showed that for women, blood sugar control could actually get worse after going on the intermittent fast for a few weeks. It's recommended to talk to your physician before starting any kind of diet plan.

Simplifies Life

While this may not be considered a health benefit like the others, it is still an important one to mention. Many people find that intermittent fasting can make their lives easier. They find that they do not need to focus as much on the calories they are eating as long as they stay within the hours that they are allowed to eat. This means that they can go a few days a week without having to worry about making a meal. Overall, this diet plan can make your life easier.

When you can cut out some of the work that you need to do during the day and focus on other things, you end up with less stress in your life. We all know how too much stress can have a negative impact on our health and life, so when you can reduce stress, it is much easier to be the healthiest version of yourself.

Good for the Heart

Heart disease is considered one of the biggest killers in the world. Intermittent fasting can help with some of these risk factors, such as lowering blood sugar levels, inflammatory markers, blood triglycerides, cholesterol, and blood pressure.

The biggest issue is that a lot of studies on intermittent fasting have been done on animals. For more conclusive results, there need to be more studies that test intermittent fasting and the heart health in humans.

Can Help with Cancer

Many people suffer from cancer each year, a disease that is characterized by uncontrolled growth of cells. Fasting has been shown to have some great benefits when it comes to your metabolism, which could lead to a reduced risk of cancer.

Some human studies show that cancer patients who fasted were able to reduce some of the side effects that come with chemotherapy.

Good for the Brain

What is considered good for the body is good for the brain as well. Intermittent fasting can help to improve metabolic features that are known for helping the brain to stay healthy as well. This could include helping with insulin resistance, blood sugar level reduction, reduced inflammation, and oxidative stress.

There have been several studies done on rats that show how intermittent fasting can help increase the growth of new nerve cells, thus helping to improve the brain's function. Fasting can also help to increase the levels of the brain-derived neurotrophic factor. When the brain is deficient in this, it can cause depression along with some other brain issues.

Helps with Cellular Repair

When we go on a fast, the cells in our bodies can initiate a waste removal process that is known as autophagy. This involves the breakdown of cells and the metabolization of any proteins that can no longer be used. With an increased amount of autophagy, it could help protect the body against diseases such as Alzheimer's and cancer.

May Prevent Alzheimer's

Alzheimer's is one of the most common neurodegenerative diseases, and while there is no cure for Alzheimer's, the best course of action is to prevent it from happening. One study that was done on rats showed that intermittent fasting might be able to delay the onset of Alzheimer's disease, or at least reduce the severity of it.

Additionally, some studies have shown that a lifestyle alteration, including some daily, or at least frequent, short-term fasts helped to improve the symptoms of Alzheimer's in 9 out of 10 patients. Other animal studies have also shown that this kind of fasting could help to protect against other neurodegenerative diseases such as Huntington's disease and Parkinson's.

While most of these studies have been done on animals, the results look promising. Intermittent fasting is a trend, and studies on the ways that it makes your body healthier are relatively new, so it will take some time to study all the benefits of intermittent fasting.

Intermittent Fasting Could Help You to Live Longer

One of the most exciting things about intermittent fasting is that it can help you live longer. There have been several rat studies that showed how intermittent fasting could help extend their lifespan - like what happens when you go on a continuous calorie restriction. In some of the studies, the effects were dramatic. For example, in one of them, when the rats fasted every other day, they ended up living 83 percent longer than the rats who didn't do fasting.

Although it has been hard to prove that intermittent fasting can help increase one's lifespan because the effects on humans have yet to be studied long enough to determine this, it is still a popular idea for those who are trying to prevent aging. Given that there are known benefits to metabolism with this diet, it is no wonder that people believe that intermittent fasting will able to help them live longer and healthier lives.

As you can see, there are lots of benefits of going with the intermittent fasting diet. We only touched on a few of them, but there have been many studies done on the effects of this diet and why/how it can benefit you. Whether you are trying to improve your brain health, live longer, lose weight, or get more energy, intermittent fasting can improve your life.

Chapter 5: Fasting, Training, and Eating

A lot of people will see results with intermittent fasting on its own. They do a good job of eating during certain windows, and when they eat, they make sure that their food is full of nutrition. However, if you would like to enhance your results and burn extra fat, then it is important to add some workouts to your routine. This chapter will take a look at the steps that you should take to properly train and exercise while on the intermittent fast.

In fact, a study recently conducted by a Sport and Health Sciences institute in Sweden shows that reducing the overall number of carbs in your diet allows your body to burn calories more effectively while also increasing your muscle growth potential. In this study, ten elite level cyclists went through an hour of interval training, going at about sixty-four percent of their maximal aerobic capacity. Additionally, they either had low or normal muscle glycogen levels that were achieved before diet or exercise intervention.

Ten muscle biopsies were taken before exercise and again three hours after they were done. The results showed that exercising while in a glycogen depleted state was able to increase mitochondrial biogenesis. This is the process by which new mitochondria can form inside the cells. The authors of the study believe that exercising on a low glycogen level diet may be beneficial for improving muscle oxidative capacity.

Part of what makes working out when you are in a fasted state effective is that the body has some mechanisms which help to preserve and protect the muscles from wasting itself. So, if you are low on fuel for a workout (which you naturally will be when you are on an intermittent fast), your body will start to break down some of the other tissues, but not the active muscle(s) that you're using.

Exercising While Preserving Your Muscles

Many experts agree that about eighty percent of the health benefits that you gain from a healthy lifestyle comes from your diet while the rest comes from exercise. This means that you need to focus on eating the right foods if you want to actually lose weight. However, it is also important to realize that both exercise and eating well are necessary.

Researchers studied data from 11 participants who were on the show, "The Biggest Loser" where participants' total body fat, total energy expenditure, and resting metabolic rate were measured three times; these were measured at the start of the program, after six weeks, and then at 30 weeks. Using a model of the human metabolism, researchers were able to calculate the impact of diet and exercise changes in resulting in weight loss to see how each one contributed to this goal.

Researchers found that diet alone was responsible for most of the weight loss; however, only about sixty-five percent of that weight loss was from body fat. The rest of the reduction in body weight was from lean muscle mass. Exercise alone resulted in fat loss only, along with a slight increase in lean muscle mass.

According to the National Institutes of Health, "The simulations also suggest that the participants could sustain their weight loss and avoid weight regain by adopting more moderate lifestyle changes – like 20 minutes of vigorous daily exercise and 20 percent calorie restriction – than those demonstrated on the television program."

Exercising and Fasting Together

If you are trying to find an effective exercise program that will add some high-intensity training in addition to intermittent fasting, there are a few components that will need to come together. When you are doing this, if you feel that you do not have enough energy to keep going with the workouts, then it is time to make a change. One way to do this is by reducing how many hours you fast. Intermittent fasting is meant to make you feel great, and if it doesn't, then it is time to change your strategy.

There are two main points that you need to keep in mind when working out while on an intermittent fast. The first is about the timing of your meals. Intermittent fasting is not all about extreme calorie restrictions as you are not meant to starve yourself to achieve great results. Rather, it is simply a matter of timing your meals properly so that you do not eat during your fasting period. You can eat during a small window, perhaps on the evening or later part of the day, so if you limit your eating to between 4pm and 7pm, you will be fasting for 21 hours.

It is ideal for most people to fast between 12 to 18 hours, though, most people prefer to fast for 16 hours because it is the easiest to fit into their busy schedules. You can find out what works the best for your needs while ensuring that you will get all of the benefits.

If you are having trouble completely abstaining from food during the day, then you may want to limit your eating to a small serving of light, low-glycemic foods. These include healthy options like poached eggs, whey protein, vegetables, and fruits every four to six hours. Regardless of whatever times you decide to eat, it's best to avoid food at least three hours before you go to bed. Doing this will help you minimize the oxidative damage in your system and can really make intermittent fasting easier to accomplish.

It's also important that break your fasts with a recovery meal on the days that you work out. On the days that you have to exercise while fasting, you need to consume a recovery meal about 30 minutes after you're done working out. Adding fast-assimilating whey protein to your meal can help with muscle recovery.

After you have had that meal, it's a good idea to fast again until you eat your main meal that night. It's important to eat an appropriate recovery meal after each workout session to help ensure that your body gets the energy that it needs, but also so that that muscle and brain damage do not occur. Do not skip this meal and make sure that you are getting it within 30 minutes after your workout.

If you think that fasting for 12 to 18 hours is difficult to accomplish, it is possible to get the same benefits from exercise and fasting by skipping breakfast and exercising right away in the morning when your stomach is empty. This is because eating a big meal before a workout, especially one that is carb-heavy, inhibits the sympathetic nervous system and reduces the fat burning effects of your exercise.

While most people have been taught that they need to take in a lot of carbs before a workout to get endurance and see results, this works against the goals that you have. Eating too many carbs activates the parasympathetic nervous system that promotes energy storage and stores calories and carbs inside the body. This is likely the last thing that you want if you are exercising and on the intermittent fast, so it's best to fast to see better results.

Tips for Getting the Most Out of Your Workouts

Working out on an intermittent fast is not meant to be hard. Exercise and plenty of physical movement are meant to help you feel good, build muscle, and lose more weight. Some of the ways that you can make sure you really do well when working out on an intermittent fast include:

- **Start out slow** – If you have never done an exercise program before, you will need to start out slowly. Even if you are just returning to an existing exercise routine, it is important to remember the changes you have made and take it slow until you know how they will affect your performance.

- **Add more weight when you feel comfortable** – in terms of weightlifting, it is important to consistently add on more weights when you start to feel comfortable. Over time, the weights that you began your workout with will start to feel lighter, and if you don't make some changes, you will find that your results will slow down. This doesn't mean that you should force your body past its limits, but it does mean you will want to regularly increase the difficulty of your exercise routine if you hope to see continued success.

- **Fewer reps and more weight is best for lean muscles** – If you are looking to build lean muscle, consider doing fewer repetitions at a higher weight. This can exhaust the body faster and will give you better results.

- **Don't forget to warmup and cool down** – Changing your eating habits doesn't give you an excuse to cut out the warmup and cooldown portions of your exercise routine. Taking at least five minutes at the start and conclusion of the workout to stretch your muscles will not only improve your performance, it will also reduce the likelihood of injury.

- **Focus on form**—Sometimes, we get too focused on how much weight we can lift when working out at the gym, but having proper form has been proven to be more important. It is better to do an exercise with the right form with lower weight than it is to add on more weight and do it poorly.

Chapter 6: The Basics of Eating on an Intermittent Fast

Eating on the intermittent fast can be as simple or as complicated as you choose to make it. Some people will continue with their healthy eating ahead of time, and others will add another type of diet to this one to see results. For example, the ketogenic diet can work well with this option because it helps to limit your carbs to reduce hunger and burn fat more quickly. However, it's not essential for you to go on any one specific diet plan to see results when on an intermittent fast.

The first thing to keep in mind is that it is not recommended that you eat unhealthy food when you are on this kind of diet plan. It is good to cut down your window of eating during the day to eight hours or less (or to do one of the other options for intermittent fasting), but, if you spend that time eating desserts, fast food, and other unhealthy foods, you will run into problems.

First, you will not be able to lose weight when you eat this way. Fast foods and other unhealthy choices come with many calories and sugar per serving, and it's likely that you are taking in more than one serving at a time. So, even though your window for eating is smaller, you can still take in too many calories which will stop all your weight loss progress. Even though intermittent fasting is not about the calorie intake, you still need to be cautious about eating too many calories because it's an aspect that can ultimately affect the effectiveness of intermittent fasting.

You will also notice that when you eat these unhealthy foods, even while on an intermittent fast, that you will not improve your health. Your health relies on good food that is high in nutrients to keep you strong. If you're simply fasting while still eating unhealthy food, this will likely cause just as many problems as you encountered before you started fasting.

When you eat these bad foods, you will find that you are hungry more often and you will struggle with getting through your fasting periods. This is because many processed and fast foods contain chemicals and preservatives that are designed to make you hungry more often. If you want to see results and get through your fast without feeling hungry, then it is time to eat foods that are better for you.

Now, this doesn't mean that you can't eat sweets or junk food occasionally. In fact, the intermittent fast doesn't have set rules for exactly what you can eat; it simply sets the times that you are allowed to eat. Eating a small cheat meal is fine if you have it during your eating windows and only do it on occasion. It may be hard sometimes but eating healthier will give you better results.

The trick to making the intermittent fast work for you is to eat a healthy diet. The more nutrients you can fit into your diet plan, the better you will end up doing with this fast.

The first thing that you need to consider is eating plenty of fruits and vegetables. Fresh produce is best because it provides lots of essential nutrients that your body needs to stay healthy. Consider filing your plate with fruits and vegetables each meal so that you are getting the nutrients that you need. Eating a wide variety of produce is also important to ensure that you are getting what your body needs without adding in too many calories.

Next, you should go with some good sources of protein. You should consider going with options like lean ground beef, turkey, and chicken. Having some bacon and other fatty meats on occasion is fine, just don't overdo it. Additionally, eating a lot of fish will help you to get the healthy fatty acids that the body needs to function properly.

Healthy sources of dairy also help you to stay lean while giving your body the calcium it needs. You can have some options such as milk, yogurt (be careful of the kinds that have fruit and other things added because these usually include a high amount of sugar), sour cream, cheese, etc., and be sure to monitor the salts and sugars that are not healthy for the body.

You can also have carbs on this diet. Recently, carbs have gotten a bit of a bad reputation because so many diet plans recommend that you avoid them, but the important thing here is to eat the carbs that are healthy for you. White bread and pasta are basically sugar in disguise and should be avoided, but choosing whole grain and whole wheat options when it comes to your carbs will ensure that you get all the nutrition that you need without all the "bad" carbs.

Having a well-balanced diet will be the key to ensuring that you feel good when you are on an intermittent fast. You will be able to mix up the meals that you choose so that you get the best results when you go on this kind of a fast.

You are also allowed to have a snack and treats as long as you are careful with how often this happens. If you are eating junk, you will be disappointed when you go to the scale and see that you are not losing weight.

Using the Ketogenic Diet with Intermittent Fasting

Lots of people decide to go on a ketogenic diet while doing an intermittent fast to help stay healthy. The ketogenic diet is a high fat, moderate protein, and low carb diet that will help you to burn fat quickly while reducing your dependence on carbs. There is a lot to love with this diet plan, and when it is combined with the intermittent fasting, you are sure to get some great results in no time.

It's possible to use both of these diet plans together. Intermittent fasting is focused on the times of day when you will eat, while the ketogenic diet on what to eat during those time periods. For those who would like to balance their blood sugar level and lose weight more efficiently, combining these two diet plans together can be a great option.

With intermittent fasting, you are limiting the hours that you eat. Instead of spreading your meals and your snacks throughout the day, you will limit it to just a few hours. Many people choose to only eat between 10am and 6pm and fit their macronutrients into that time. Others, however, will take two or three days during the week where they are not allowed to eat and fit their nutrients into the other days of the week.

The point is that you are limiting the amount of time that you eat, thereby forcing yourself to think more about the foods you consume. You also get the benefit of more fat burning and weight loss, when you do intermittent fasting.

During your non-fasting times, you will need to stick with the macronutrients that we discussed above that are approved for the ketogenic diet. This means that you will still stick with high fat, moderate protein, and low carb diet plan even while intermittent fasting. You will just need to be more careful about the times you eat those macronutrients, but otherwise, you can follow the ketogenic diet exactly the same.

If you want to get some of the benefits of intermittent fasting or want to increase your weight loss, then adding this diet in with the ketogenic diet can be effective. You can experiment with the different types of intermittent fasting options that are available to see which one fits into your schedule the best or works the best for you. Of course, if you find the ketogenic diet is effective or intermittent fasting is too difficult, you can always just stick with the ketogenic diet and not fast and still see good results.

It is important to remember that you don't have to follow the ketogenic diet if you don't want to while on an intermittent fast. Many people do choose other healthy diets over the ketogenic diet, but many still choose to go with the ketogenic diet along with intermittent fasting because it is easy to follow and will allow them to lose even more fat.

Eating on the intermittent fast does not need to be too difficult. You can pick out the foods that you want to eat, although it is important to go with foods that are fresh and whole and will fill you up and help with the fat burning process to help you to see the weight loss that you are looking for.

Chapter 7: Basic Tips for Intermittent Fasting

Getting started with intermittent fasting can take some time because you will have to change some of the eating patterns that you are used to, but it can be effective for you in so many ways. You will see that it is easier to lose weight, can improve your energy, burn body fat, help you to get more done, and help to protect you against diseases such as diabetes, cancer, and dementia.

Although intermittent fasting is easier than many other diet plans out there, it still takes some work. Some of the things to keep in mind to get the most out of your intermittent fast are:

- **Drink plenty of water:** Water keeps you hydrated and makes you feel fuller when you are on your fast. Being in a fasted state also acts as a diuretic, which means that your body will naturally expel water at a faster rate than you are used to. For best results, it's recommended that you drink a gallon of water.

- **Drink tea and coffee:** When you are feeling hungry, you may find that it's helpful to drink tea or coffee to keep down your appetite. Caffeine is a natural appetite suppressant, but be mindful and try not to consume any caffeine too close to bedtime (at least 3 hours), or you may have trouble falling asleep.

- **Keep yourself busy:** You may find that you are more productive on an empty stomach. If you are keeping yourself busy, not only will you get more done, but you'll be able to distract yourself from the hunger. If you don't find productive ways to fill your time, especially at first, then you will find that the hours you are fasting seem to stretch out into days. Don't make things harder on yourself than they need to be. When it comes to the early days of your new diet, make sure your days are packed full of activities.

- **Make it flexible:** There are so many options that come with intermittent fasting so remember that you do not have to go with one option because everyone else is. You can mix and match and create the schedule that works for you. Intermittent fasting is all about having the freedom to do it the way that you want.

- **Try it for at least a month:** You need at least three to four weeks to determine if the intermittent fast is right for you. If you don't do it for at least this long, then you are not giving the body the time it needs to adapt. More importantly, you are not giving yourself a fair shot. Try it out for at least a month to see if it's the right choice for you.

- **Experiment with fasting methods:** What works for one person may not work for you. If you find that certain fasting times are better or that a particular version of intermittent fasting is more effective, then choose those. It's all experimenting to see what feels right for you.

- **Delay your breakfast slowly:** One thing that works well for a lot of people is to slowly delay their breakfast. By gradually pushing back your breakfast time an hour every week or so, you will eventually get yourself into an intermittent fast without it being too difficult. For instance, if you usually eat breakfast at 8 am, wait until 8:30 am to eat your breakfast for the first week. Then, push your breakfast back to 9 am in week 2. Continue this process until your first meal occurs around 12 pm.

- **Drink water in the morning:** Oftentimes, the reason that you feel so hungry in the morning is that you have gone all night without eating. A good habit to pick up is to drink a glass of water right when you wake up in the morning.

- **Add weights:** If you are trying to lose weight and tone up, it makes sense to add some weight training to your routine. While you won't want to mix things up too much when you are first getting started, once your body has adapted to an intermittent fasting lifestyle, there is no reason you shouldn't take things up a notch. You will be surprised what your body can handle. If you take things slowly, eventually you should be able to handle a full-intensity workout without feeling too drained to function when you are finished.

- **Live it up:** With intermittent fasting, you need to realize that you can live it up on occasion as long as you ensure it all balances out in the end. While the average diet is all about the foods that you aren't allowed to eat, an intermittent fasting lifestyle accounts for the fact that you simply can't plan your meals sometimes. This means that as long as you get your fasting period in, there is no reason you can't move your hours around... as long as you don't do so constantly. Additionally, there is no reason you can't indulge now and again, as long as one delicious and decadent dessert doesn't end up turning into seven or eight.

- **Get out of the house:** There is a lot of temptation in your home, therefore, it is better to get out of the house so that you don't eat all that food. Even if you have kids around, think of an activity you all can do to keep yourselves occupied.

- **Eat more protein and healthy fats:** Eating additional protein with each meal makes it easier to control your appetite and build up your muscles. Eating more healthy fat will give you extra energy and help you feel fuller longer as well. Thanks to the insidious advancement of the Standard

American Diet, a vast majority of those in the Western world eat far too many carbohydrates and not nearly enough protein or healthy fat. To rectify this problem, think about the macros of the foods you eat. You should also ensure that, when you are in an eating window, you fill your plate with foods that will make sticking it out to the next window as easy as possible.

- **Avoid the bad stuff:** You need to make sure that you are not using your non-fasting period as an excuse to eat junk food all the time. Make sure to stick with a well-balanced diet so that you provide your body with enough nutrition, even if you choose to go on a fast. It is important to keep in mind that a big part of intermittent fasting is building up a calorie deficit by the end of the week to support additional weight loss. As such, if you fill your body full of high-calorie junk food when you do enter an eating window, what you are really doing is undoing all of your hard work.

Making consistent healthy choices will improve the overall effectiveness of your weight loss efforts, guaranteed.

As you can see, there are a lot of different things you can do to get the most out of intermittent fasting. This doesn't mean you should expect constant weight loss, however, regardless of how strict your fasting might be. While you will likely see weight loss at first as your body adapts to fewer calories in its system; this will likely start and stop throughout your time fasting. The effects are especially noticeable after the first few weeks of the transition as your body tries to hold on to everything it has until it can figure out what is going on. Once it gets with the program, however, things should proceed as expected.

Every diet is going to have periods of weight loss plateau. That is simply a part of weight loss that cannot be mitigated. As long as you stay consistent, weight loss will eventually resume. The worst thing you can do is to try and change things to get your weight loss back on track as that will only make it more difficult for your body to start losing weight again. Instead, if you stay the course and keep up the good work, you will start seeing results again before you know it.

Chapter 8: Intermittent Fast FAQs

There are a lot of questions that you may have when it comes to intermittent fasting. You'll want to make sure that you are doing it the right way and that you will be able to get all the benefits that are promised with this diet plan. This chapter will take some time to explore more about intermittent fasting and what you need to know to get it to work for you.

Is There Anyone Who Shouldn't Fast?

For the most part, intermittent fasting is safe for most people to do. It's an effective diet plan that focuses on healthy eating and getting the essential calories and nutrition that your body needs while restricting the windows that you're allowed to eat.

With that said, some people should not go on an intermittent fast mostly because there is concern that they will not be able to get the nutrition that they need. For example, if you're considered underweight, you should not go on this kind of fast. Likewise, if you're pregnant or breastfeeding, you will need to take in nutrients throughout the day to support your child, so intermittent fasting is not the best option for you.

Additionally, there are times when you are allowed to fast, but you may want to make sure that you have some supervision from your doctor. First, if you have diabetes of any kind, you will need to do this with the help of your doctor as some medications don't work well with these fasts. You should take similar precautions if you have high uric acid or gout.

Will I go Into Starvation Mode if I am Fasting?

There are a lot of myths about fasting and they are repeated so often that they are sometimes seen as truths. Some of the fasting myths that you may know about include:

- Fasting means you are starving

- Fasting will you feel hungry

- Fasting will make you overeat when the fast is over

- Fasting will make you lose muscle tone

These myths have been disproven many times over. For instance, instead of the body going into starvation mode, it will start burning through the extra fat stores. This will help you to get rid of that stubborn belly fat and will help you become healthier, especially if you have been overeating for a long time.

Over a year, you consume about 1,000 meals and over 60 years, you will eat about 60,000 meals, so to say that skipping three meals during this time will cause a lot of harm is silly.

The breakdown of muscle tissue only occurs at low levels of body fat, so if you are already at that point, then you shouldn't go on a fast. However, most people will not have this issue as our bodies have evolved to handle periods of starvation and will be able to effectively deal with it.

What are Some Side Effects of Going on a Fast?

There are a few side effects that you can deal with when you are on a fast. These are usually minor and will go away after your body adjusts to the diet and you familiarize yourself with eating habits that work well. Some of the side effects that you may experience include:

- Constipation: This is a common side effect. If you're experiencing constipation, using laxatives can to help to alleviate the pain or discomfort.

- Headaches: Some people experience headaches when they get started on a fast, but these will disappear within a few days. A good way to deal with this is to eat a little extra salt each day.

- Stomach gurgling: If you are dealing with your stomach gurgling, then it is a good idea to use mineral water.

- Other side effects: You may also deal with issues such as muscle cramps, dizziness, and heartburn. Adjusting your diet and waiting a few days will help to alleviate any discomfort.

How Do I Manage Hunger?

The most important thing to remember is that this hunger will pass. Most people worry that their hunger will keep growing until it is intolerable, but this usually isn't the case. Hunger comes in waves, so ignoring it and drinking some water, tea, or coffee will help you to cope with the hunger pangs.

During your extended fast, you might notice that your hunger will increase into the second day. After you get past that time, you will see that it recedes, and many people report that they have a complete loss of hunger by day 3 or 4. At this time, your body is powered by fat. This means that the body is eating its own fat for breakfast, lunch, and dinner, so you are no longer feeling so hungry. So, if you can last a few days on the intermittent fast, the hunger pangs will go away, and it will be easier to deal with.

It is important to keep in mind that when you are first starting out your body is likely to struggle with fasting because it is used to have ready access to fuel at all times. Most of us are used to eating, even when we are not hungry, so your body will fight against your new habit with extreme hunger pangs in an effort to get back on track. However, whether you go with the 16/8 fast, the 5:2 fast, or the alternate day fast, the truth of the matter is that you are not putting your body through anything it cannot handle. As such, as long as you stay the course, things will likely settle down in about a week or so once your body realizes that it is not, in fact, starving.

In order to make the transition as manageable as possible, the first thing you are going to want to do is to add more caffeine to your diet. While not acceptable in the long-term, this is a great way to keep the worst of the hunger pangs away when they are at their sharpest. Additionally, you will want to ensure that your schedule is full during this time as the more activity your mind has to focus on, the faster time will fly. Finally, if you are already committed to an exercise routine, then you will want to ensure that you exercise right before you break your fast so that your body will get the fuel it needs to make the most of your efforts.

Will Fasting Burn Muscle?

This is a common misconception that a lot of people deal with when they are considering an intermittent fast. During fasting periods, the body's first response is to break down the glycogen into glucose so that it can be used for energy. After the glucose is all gone, the body will increase how much fat it's breaking down and use that for energy. Excess amino acids, which are the building blocks of protein, can also be used for energy. However, it should be noted that the body is not going to use its own muscle as fuel unless you're not eating for weeks on end.

Fasting is a practice that has been done for thousands of years. It's safe and effective, and unless you go for weeks without eating (and none of the intermittent fasting options ask you to fast for more than 24 hours), there is no reason to worry about losing excess muscle.

How Do I Break a Fast?

Breaking a fast is one of the hardest parts of this diet and is likely the truest test of whether you will be able to sustain it in long-term. When you break your fast, it is important to do so in moderation for multiple reasons. First, it is important to not add too much back into your system all at once as this can put stress on your body, damaging your stomach and intestines if repeated too often. Additionally, if you allow yourself to gorge when your resolve is at its weakest, then you are far more likely to overeat and undue all the hard work you have done by fasting in the first place.

The best way to ensure that this does not happen is to plan ahead. Prepare the meal while you are waiting for the fast to end and ensure that it has very clearly defined portions. A hearty omelet is a good choice as you can fill it full of healthy, filling items and you can't easily go back for seconds. Meanwhile, a full pot of oatmeal is a poor choice as you could easily go through it without thinking twice.

Can Women Fast?

Yes, women can fast and the only exceptions to this rule are if you're underweight, pregnant, or breastfeeding. This is because your body needs those extra nutrients and should not go so long without eating in these situations. Other than that, it is perfectly fine for women to fast. In addition, the average weight loss with fasting is the same for men and women so it can be effective for both genders.

Tips for Intermittent Fasting

Getting started with intermittent fasting can be challenging at times. To summarize, tips you can follow include:

- Drink lots of water

- Stay busy

- Drink coffee or tea to suppress hunger

- Find a good support group that can help you

- Ride out the hunger waves because they will go away

- Try to go on a low-carb diet as it will help you with reducing hunger and can make fasting easier; it can also help out with more weight loss.

- Try it out for a month

- Break your fast gently

- Do not binge when you are done with fasting

Final Thoughts

Intermittent fasting is a great option if you want to burn fat, lose weight, and get in better shape. This diet is not only about the foods that you eat, but about the time of the day that you eat these foods so that you can be healthy by getting your body to do the hard work for you.

The hardest part of this diet is to teach yourself to not eat all the time. We have been taught that we need to eat five or six (small) meals a day, but this isn't the case for most people. With intermittent fasting, you will be able to get the results that you need without having to work so hard.

Intermittent fasting is not just a weight-loss diet – it aims for more than that. It has several health benefits that will not only make you slimmer but also healthier and disease-free.

Conclusion

Thanks for making it through to the end of this book. I hope that it was informative and able to provide you with all of the tools you need to achieve your health and fitness goals.

The next step is to get started on your journey with intermittent fasting. Intermittent fasting offers many benefits for your body, so whether you are looking to lose weight or improve your health, intermittent fasting is the way to go.

There are a lot of options that come with intermittent fasting, so you can pick the option that will work the best for you. Intermittent fasting is simple, easy to work with, and effective. When you are ready to lose weight and improve your health, refer back to this guidebook to help you get started.

Appendix

Coming up with a proper meal plan you can follow on your fasting days can be challenging with an intermittent fast. Here are some great meal plans you can follow to help make the intermittent fast work best for you.

Fast Day Plan 1

Breakfast: Quaker Oats sachet of porridge (40g) - 255 calories

Dinner: Beetroot and feta salad - 125 calories

- Beetroot (50g) - 13 calories

- Feta (30g) - 83 calories

- Spinach (60g) - 29 calories

- A squeeze of lemon - 0 calories

Snack: Sliced apple with 1 tbsp. of almond butter - 145 calories

Total calorie count: 525

Fast Day Plan 2

Breakfast: Sweet plums and yogurt - 145 calories

- 100g low-fat natural yogurt - 65 calories

- 2 plums - 60 calories

- 1 tsp of honey - 20 calories

Dinner: Ryvita and tuna slices - 253 calories

- 2 x original Ryvita crackerbreads - 70 calories

- Tuna mayo (60g) - 171 calories

- Rocket (70g) sprinkled on top - 12 calories

- cracked black pepper - 0 calories

Snack: Miso soup - 32 calories

Total calorie count: 430

Fast Day Plan 3

Breakfast: Soft boiled egg and asparagus - 90 calories

- 1 egg - 70 calories

- 5 pieces of asparagus - 20 calories

- salt and pepper to season

Dinner: Turkey burgers with corn-on-the-cob - 328 calories

- Minced turkey with beaten small egg, spring onion, garlic and chili (111g) - 172 calories

- 1 x corn-on-the-cob - 156 calories

Snack: A few frozen grapes - 60 calories

Total calorie count: 478 calories

<u>Fast Day Plan 4</u>

Breakfast: Packet of Belvita Breakfast Biscuits (muesli) - 228 calories

Dinner: Roasted vegetables with balsamic glaze - 261 calories

- ½ courgette, ½ aubergine, ½ butternut squash, ½ red pepper - 247

- 1 tbsp. balsamic vinegar - 14 calories

- A squeeze of lemon - 0 calories

Snack: Harley's sugar-free jelly pot - 4 calories

Total calorie count: 493

Fast Day Plan 5

Breakfast: Spinach omelet - 160

- 2 x eggs - 140

- Spinach leaves (60g) - 20

- Salt and pepper - no calories

Dinner: Hummus and crudités - 175 calories

- Hummus (40g) - 123 calories

- A medium bowl full of carrots, cucumber, raw pepper - 52 calories

Snack: Edamame beans (60g) and rock salt - 84 calories

Total calorie count: 419

Fast Day Plan 6

Breakfast: Banana and low-fat yogurt - 177 calories

- 100g low-fat natural yogurt - 65 calories

- 1 x banana - 112 calories

- A sprinkle of cinnamon - 0 calories

Dinner: Turkey breasts with wilted spinach - 216 calories

- 1 x turkey breast steak (125g) - 175 calories

- 1 cup of spinach, cooked and seasoned with salt - 41 calories

Snack: 10g of popcorn - 59 calories

Total calorie count: 452

Fast Day Plan 7

Breakfast: Apple, carrot, and ginger smoothie - 107 calories

- 1 apple - 55 calories

- 1 carrot - 52

- raw ginger - 0 calories

Dinner: Pitta pizza - 178 calories

- Weight Watchers whole meal pitta - 106 calories

- 25g Extra Light Philadelphia cheese - 40 calories

- 1 tomato - 32 calories

- Mixed herbs - 0 calories

- Salt and pepper - 0 calories

Snack: 100g blueberries and a handful of almonds - 137 calories

Total calorie count: 422

Review Request

If you enjoyed this book or found it useful, then I'd like to ask you for a quick favor: would you be kind enough to leave a review for this book on Amazon? It'd be greatly appreciated.

Your feedback does matter and helps me to make improvements so I can provide the best content possible. Thank you!

You can leave a review at:

http://bit.ly/artoffasting

Further reading

The Science of Intermittent Fasting: The Complete Guide to Unlocking Your Weight Loss Potential

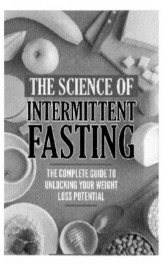

Are you thinking about losing weight or have you been trying to lose weight unsuccessfully?

Are you ready to try something that will shed those excess pounds and boost your heath?

In ***The Science of Intermittent Fasting,*** you can discover how intermittent fasting could work for you, through chapters that look at:

- What intermittent fasting is all about
- Cellular repair
- Improving brain health
- Optimizing your insulin, leptin and ghrelin levels
- Inflammation

- Cholesterol
- Cancer and diabetes
- Aging
- How to get the most out of your fasts
- And lots more…

The scientific benefits of intermittent fasting on your health and weight loss are clear to see and with an in-depth look into the research and studies carried out on intermittent fasting, ***The Science of Intermittent Fasting*** is the perfect book that deliver all the answers.

Get a copy today and see for yourself how intermittent fasting can not only be good for your weight, but good for your whole body.

Get your copy now at:

http://bit.ly/thescienceoffastingbook

The Ultimate Fasting Diet: Simple Intermittent Fasting Strategies to Boost Weight Loss, Control Hunger, Fight Disease, and Slow Down Aging

The Ultimate Fasting Diet will show you everything that you need to know in order to eat properly and succeed on the intermittent fast. It also come with 28 easy, quick, delicious recipes to use for your fasting and nonfasting days.

Some of the topics that we will discuss include:

- Why is your diet failing you?
- What is the intermittent fast?
- The Scientific benefits of Intermittent Fasting
- Facts and myths about intermittent fasting
- Things to keep in mind for your Fasting vs. Non-Fasting Days
- Foods allowed on the intermittent fast

- 28 Delicious easy quick recipes for your fasting and non fastings days
- Easy breakfast recipes
- Easy lunch recipes
- Dinner recipes with protein to fill you up
- Tasty snacks for any time
- A 7-day meal plan to get started with intermittent fasting
- FAQs about fasting to ensure you succeed
- And more...

Are you ready to lose weight and feel better once and for all?

Get your copy now here:

http://bit.ly/ultimatefastingdiet

Fasting Resources

- https://www.psychologytoday.com/blog/food-junkie/201308/the-american-diet
- https://www.healthline.com/nutrition/what-is-intermittent-fasting#section4
- https://www.healthline.com/nutrition/intermittent-fasting-guide#modal-close
- https://www.sciencedirect.com/science/article/pii/S193152441400200X
- http://ibimapublishing.com/articles/ENDO/2014/459119/
- https://www.ncbi.nlm.nih.gov/pmc/articles/PMC3946160/
- https://www.ncbi.nlm.nih.gov/pmc/articles/PMC3106288/
- https://www.ncbi.nlm.nih.gov/pubmed/25540982
- https://www.ncbi.nlm.nih.gov/pubmed/2405717
- https://www.karger.com/Article/Abstract/212538
- http://www.aging-us.com/article/100690

- https://www.ncbi.nlm.nih.gov/pubmed/17306 982
- https://fitness.mercola.com/sites/fitness/archi ve/2012/11/02/interval-training-and-intermittent-fasting.aspx
- http://www.thefatlossninja.com/top-17-intermittent-fasting-tricks/

96247990R00059

Made in the USA
Middletown, DE
31 October 2018